United States Government Accountability Office

Report to Congressional Committees

I0448464

June 2013

DEFENSE ACQUISITIONS

Goals and Associated Metrics Needed to Assess Progress in Improving Service Acquisition

GAO Highlights

Highlights of GAO-13-634, a report to congressional committees

DEFENSE ACQUISITIONS

Goals and Associated Metrics Needed to Assess Progress in Improving Service Acquisition

Why GAO Did This Study

In fiscal year 2012, DOD obligated more than $186 billion for contracted services, making it the federal government's largest buyer of services. GAO's prior work found that DOD's use of contracted services has been the result of thousands of individual decisions, not strategic planning across the department.

Over the years, Congress has legislated a number of requirements to improve DOD's service acquisitions. For example, Congress required DOD to implement a service acquisition management structure, approval process, and policies. Congress also directed DOD to develop a plan to implement the Defense Science Board's recommendations for improving service acquisition.

The National Defense Authorization Act for Fiscal Year 2012 mandated that GAO report on DOD's actions to improve service acquisition and management. GAO examined (1) the actions DOD has taken to respond to legislative requirements and (2) how DOD determines the effects of its actions to improve service acquisition. GAO reviewed documentation and interviewed DOD officials on the actions taken in response to the legislative requirements. GAO also assessed whether DOD addressed key factors, including establishing goals and metrics, to help it determine if it has improved service acquisition.

What GAO Recommends

GAO recommends that DOD establish baseline data, specific goals for improving service acquisition, and associated metrics to assess its progress. DOD concurred with the three recommendations.

View GAO-13-634. For more information, contact Timothy J. DiNapoli at (202) 512-4841 or dinapolit@gao.gov.

What GAO Found

Over the last decade, the Department of Defense (DOD) has taken several actions to address legislative requirements to improve the acquisition and management of services. In 2001, as amended in 2006, Congress required DOD to implement a management structure for the acquisition of services. In response, DOD implemented such a structure and service acquisition review and approval process. Recently, DOD also established new positions within its management structure, including senior managers within the office of the Under Secretary of Defense for Acquisition, Technology, and Logistics (USD(AT&L)) and the military departments, to oversee and coordinate service acquisition. With a management structure and review process in place, USD(AT&L) is focusing on efforts to improve the process for how requirements for individual service acquisitions are developed and enhancing training to respond to several legislative directives. USD(AT&L) also created its Acquisition of Services Functional Integrated Product Team, in part, to determine how to address legislative requirements to provide training for personnel acquiring services. USD(AT&L) did not develop a plan to implement the Defense Science Board recommendations to improve service acquisition but identified 23 different actions, including its Better Buying Power Initiative, it has planned or taken that officials regard as addressing what the plan was to include. For example, USD(AT&L) is updating its guidance on using incentives to improve contractor performance, which addresses one of the elements that was to be in the plan.

While DOD has taken a number of actions that address legislative requirements, DOD is not yet positioned to determine what effects these actions have had on improving service acquisition. Specifically, USD(AT&L) has not identified specific goals and associated metrics that would enable it to assess progress toward achieving those goals. USD(AT&L) has identified improving service acquisition as a priority but has not defined a desired end state for its actions or the measurable characteristics that would embody achieving such a goal. It is challenged in defining a desired end state for its actions, in part, because it has not determined the current status of service acquisition in terms of the volume, type, location, and trends. DOD is taking steps to improve its contract and financial systems to obtain such data, but these efforts will not be complete until at least 2014. Further, DOD has not established departmentwide metrics to assess its progress in improving service acquisition but has acknowledged the need to do so, which officials described as challenging. Nevertheless, despite the challenges in doing so, it is not impossible. For example, DOD has agreed to set goals for the amount of spending managed through strategically sourced acquisitions, link strategic sourcing to its Better Buying Power Initiative, and establish metrics, such as utilization rates, to track progress toward these goals. However, DOD is not fully leveraging the command-level assessments, feedback from the military departments, and other ongoing efforts it relies on to gauge the effects of its actions to improve service acquisition. By using its budget and spending data and leveraging these efforts, DOD could develop baseline data and identify trends over time, enabling it to develop measurable goals and gain more insight into whether its actions are improving service acquisition. Until then, DOD will continue to be in a position where it does not know whether its actions are sufficient to achieve desired outcomes.

_____ **United States Government Accountability Office**

Contents

Abbreviations

ARRT	Acquisition Requirements Roadmap Tool
Services FIPT	Acquisition of Services Functional Integrated Product Team
COR	Contracting Officer's Representative
DAU	Defense Acquisition University
DAWDF	Defense Acquisition Workforce Development Fund
DPAP	Defense Procurement and Acquisition Policy
DSB	Defense Science Board
DOD	Department of Defense
FPDS-NG	Federal Procurement Data System-Next Generation
NDAA	National Defense Authorization Act
SAW	Services Acquisition Workshop
USD(AT&L)	Under Secretary of Defense for Acquisition, Technology, and Logistics

June 27, 2013

Congressional Committees

Since fiscal year 2000, the Department of Defense's (DOD) annual obligations for contracted services have more than doubled when adjusted for inflation. In fiscal year 2012, DOD reported $186 billion in obligations for contracted services, making the department the federal government's largest buyer of contracted services. DOD buys a wide range of services, including consulting, administrative, medical, and information technology, to support its missions. Within DOD, responsibility for acquiring these services is spread among buying activities within individual military commands, weapon system program offices, and functional units on military bases. We previously found the increased use of contracted services has been the result of thousands of individual decisions, not strategic planning across the department.[1]

Congress has passed a number of measures over the years to improve DOD's acquisition and management of contracted services. In 2001, Congress required the Secretary of Defense to establish a management structure for the acquisition of services, under section 2330, title 10, United States Code.[2] As part of the management structure, the Secretary was to designate officials within the military departments and defense agencies to be responsible for managing service acquisition within their respective departments or agencies. The Secretary was also directed to establish a process for approving individual service acquisitions in advance of contract award. Congress subsequently amended 10 U.S.C. § 2330 in 2006 to require, among other things, that the Under Secretary of Defense for Acquisition, Technology, and Logistics (USD(AT&L)) develop and maintain policies, procedures, and best practices guidelines

---

[1] GAO, *Defense Acquisitions: Further Actions Needed to Address Weaknesses in DOD's Management of Professional and Management Support Contracts*, GAO-10-39 (Washington, D.C.: Nov. 20, 2009). Over the years, we have made numerous recommendations to improve DOD's acquisition of services. Information on these recommendations and their status is presented later in this report, as appropriate.

[2] National Defense Authorization Act for Fiscal Year 2002, Pub. L. No. 107-107, § 801(b) (2001).

for acquisition planning, requirements development, and other aspects involved with the procurement of contracted services.[3]

More recently, in section 802 of the National Defense Authorization Act (NDAA) for Fiscal Year 2010, Congress required USD(AT&L) to have the Defense Science Board (DSB) independently assess improvements to DOD's acquisition and oversight of services.[4] The resulting March 2011 DSB report contained multiple recommendations to improve DOD's approach to contracting for services.[5] The DSB's recommendations focused on creating new policies and processes, strengthening management and oversight, designating roles and leadership responsibilities, and improving the skills and capabilities of personnel involved in services contracting. Subsequently, as part of section 807 of the NDAA for Fiscal Year 2012, Congress directed USD(AT&L) to develop a plan for implementing the recommendations of the DSB to include, to the extent USD(AT&L) deemed appropriate, eight elements, most of which align with the DSB's recommendations.[6] These eight elements include incentives for high contractor performance, guidance on the use of appropriate contract types, and training of services acquisition personnel.

Section 807 of the NDAA for Fiscal Year 2012 also mandated that we report on DOD's actions to improve service acquisition and management.[7] This report addresses (1) DOD's actions to address legislative requirements in 10 U.S.C. § 2330 and section 807 and (2) the extent to which DOD is able to determine whether its actions have resulted in improvements to service acquisition and management.

To describe how DOD has addressed legislative requirements, we reviewed policies, guidance, memorandums, and additional information

---

[3]National Defense Authorization Act for Fiscal Year 2006, Pub. L. No. 109-163, § 812.

[4]Pub. L. No. 111-84 (2009). The Defense Science Board was established to provide independent advice and recommendations on science, technology, manufacturing, acquisition processes, and other matters of special interest to the DOD.

[5]Office of Under Secretary of Defense for Acquisition, Technology, and Logistics, *Report of the Defense Science Board Task Force on Improvements to Services Contracting* (Washington, D.C.: Mar. 8, 2011).

[6]Pub. L. No. 112-81, § 807(b) (2011).

[7]Pub. L. No. 112-81, § 807(c) (2011).

documenting the actions that USD(AT&L) and the Departments of the Air Force, Army, and Navy identified as taking in response to 10 U.S.C. § 2330 and section 807 of the NDAA for Fiscal Year 2012. We interviewed USD(AT&L) and military department officials regarding how DOD is implementing these actions. We also met with Defense Acquisition University (DAU) officials to obtain information on training, guidance, and other efforts to address legislative requirements for service acquisition training or career development.

To evaluate the extent to which DOD is able to determine whether its actions have resulted in improvements to service acquisition and management, we interviewed USD(AT&L) and senior military department officials responsible for overseeing service acquisition and management. We reviewed supporting documentation on the approaches they have used to gain insight into the effectiveness of their actions, including USD(AT&L) and the military departments' reviews of individual service acquisitions. We then assessed whether these approaches reflected key factors needed to improve service acquisition based on findings in our November 2006 report to determine if improvement efforts are achieving their intended results.[8] In the 2006 report, we identified several key factors, which we consider to still be relevant, that leading commercial firms reported must be in place to significantly improve service acquisition. These factors include (1) leadership commitment, (2) a desired end state with goals for the future, and (3) metrics that define specified outcomes. We also found that critical to establishing a desired end state with goals for the future is the ability to determine where service acquisition is today in terms of specific and aggregate knowledge on the current volume, type, location, and trends.

We conducted this performance audit from September 2012 to June 2013 in accordance with generally accepted government auditing standards. Those standards require that we plan and perform the audit to obtain sufficient, appropriate evidence to provide a reasonable basis for our findings and conclusions based on our audit objectives. We believe that the evidence obtained provides a reasonable basis for our findings and conclusions based on our audit objectives.

---

[8]GAO, *Defense Acquisitions: Tailored Approach Needed to Improve Service Acquisition Outcomes*, GAO-07-20 (Washington, D.C.: Nov. 9, 2006).

Background

Our prior work has found that DOD's approach to managing service acquisition has tended to be reactive and has not fully addressed key factors for success at either the strategic or transactional level.[9] The strategic level is where the enterprise sets the direction or vision for what it needs, captures knowledge to enable more informed management decisions, ensures enterprisewide goals and objectives are achieved, determines how to go about meeting those needs, and assesses the resources it has to achieve desired outcomes. The strategic level also sets the context for the transactional level, where the focus is on making sound decisions on individual acquisitions.

Congress has required USD(AT&L) to take a number of steps to improve service acquisition. Specifically in 10 U.S.C. § 2330, enacted in 2001 and amended in 2006, Congress required USD(AT&L) and the military departments to establish a management structure for the acquisition of services.[10] Since 2003, we have evaluated DOD's implementation of 10 U.S.C. § 2330 and efforts to establish the management structure and service acquisition approval process twice. First, in September 2003, we concluded that DOD's approach to managing service acquisition did not provide a departmentwide assessment of how spending for services could be more effective.[11] We therefore recommended that DOD give greater attention to promoting a strategic orientation by setting performance goals for improvements and ensuring accountability for results. DOD concurred in principle with our recommendation and agreed that additional actions could strengthen the management structure and acquisition approval process but also identified challenges for doing so based on its organizational size, complexity, and the acquisition environment.

Subsequently, in November 2006, we found continued weaknesses associated with DOD's management of service acquisitions at the strategic and transactional level.[12] Specifically, we found that DOD's approach to managing service acquisition tended to be reactive and that the department had not developed a means for evaluating whether

---

[9]GAO-07-20.

[10]Pub. L. No. 107-107, § 801(b); Pub. L. No. 109-163, § 812.

[11]GAO, *Contract Management: High-Level Attention Needed to Transform DOD Services Acquisition,* GAO-03-935 (Washington, D.C.: Sept. 10, 2003).

[12]GAO-07-20.

ongoing and planned efforts were achieving intended results. DOD had not developed a strategic vision and lacked sustained commitment to managing service acquisition risks and fostering more efficient outcomes. DOD also had not developed metrics to assess whether any changes to improve service acquisition actually achieved the expected outcomes. As a result, DOD was not in a position to determine whether investments in services were achieving their desired outcomes. Moreover, the results of individual acquisitions were generally not used to inform or adjust the strategic direction. We recommended that, among other actions, DOD take steps to understand how and where service acquisition dollars are currently and will be spent, in part, to assist in adopting a proactive approach to managing service acquisition. We also recommended that DOD take steps to provide a capability to determine whether service acquisitions are meeting cost, schedule, and performance objectives. At that time, DOD concurred with our recommendations. USD(AT&L), however, acknowledged in 2010 that DOD still needed a cohesive, integrated strategy for acquiring services. DOD contract management has remained on our High Risk List, in part, because DOD has not developed such a strategy and continues to lack reliable services spending data to inform decision making.[13]

While Congress has required USD(AT&L) to take steps to improve service acquisition, USD(AT&L) has taken actions on its own initiative as well. For example, USD(AT&L) established its Better Buying Power Initiative in a September 2010 memorandum to provide guidance for obtaining greater efficiency and productivity in defense spending. In its memorandum, USD(AT&L) emphasized that DOD must prepare to continue supporting the warfighter through the acquisition of products and services in potentially fiscally constrained times. In its own words, USD(AT&L) noted that DOD must "do more without more." USD(AT&L) organized the Better Buying Power Initiative around five major areas, including an area focused on improving tradecraft in service acquisition. This area identified actions to improve service acquisition, such as categorizing acquisitions by portfolio groups and assigning new managers to coordinate these groups. USD(AT&L) issued another memorandum in April 2013 to update the Better Buying Power Initiative. This memorandum identifies seven areas USD(AT&L) is pursuing to increase efficiency and productivity in defense spending. One area is to improve service acquisition and the memorandum identifies a number of related

---

[13]GAO, *High-Risk Series: An Update,* GAO-13-283 (Washington, D.C.: February 2013).

actions, such as increasing small business participation in service acquisitions and improving how DOD conducts services-related market research.

DOD Has Taken Actions to Address Legislative Requirements to Improve Service Acquisition

Over the last decade, DOD has taken actions to address legislative requirements to improve the acquisition and management of services. Senior officials we spoke with across the military departments credit USD(AT&L)'s leadership and commitment as the driving force behind many of the actions taken to improve service acquisition. A number of these actions were intended to strengthen DOD's management structure and approach to reviewing service acquisitions, as required by 10 U.S.C. § 2330. For example, both USD(AT&L) and the military departments established new senior management positions to improve oversight and coordination of service acquisition. With this management structure and review process in place, USD(AT&L) is focusing on efforts to improve the process for how requirements for individual service acquisitions are developed and training to respond to legislative direction. USD(AT&L) also created a senior-level team to identify and determine the training needs for DOD personnel responsible for developing service acquisition requirements. USD(AT&L) did not develop a specific implementation plan as required by section 807, but officials identified a number of actions that they regard as addressing the eight elements specified.

DOD Has Strengthened Its Management Structure and Service Acquisition Review Process

Since 2002, DOD has increased its management attention on high dollar value service acquisitions by instituting new policies and review processes. In response to the initial requirements to establish a management structure for the acquisition of services, USD(AT&L) issued a guidance memorandum in May 2002. This memorandum required that service acquisitions be reviewed and approved based on dollar thresholds and that the acquisition strategy—addressing things such as the requirements to be satisfied and any potential risks—be approved prior to initiating any action to commit the government to the strategy. Under this policy, USD(AT&L) was responsible for reviewing and approving all proposed service acquisitions with an estimated value of $2 billion or more. Following the 2006 amendment to 10 U.S.C. § 2330, USD(AT&L) issued a revised memorandum in October of that year. Under the revised policy, which remains in effect, USD(AT&L) lowered the threshold for its review to service acquisitions valued at over $1 billion. The military departments have developed internal policies for reviewing and approving service acquisitions below USD(AT&L)'s threshold. Further, USD(AT&L) required that acquisition strategies be reviewed before contract award and that these and other acquisition planning documents include a top-level discussion of the source selection process as well as noting any waivers and deviations. USD(AT&L) and military department officials informed us that while these reviews are conducted, they have not tracked the total number of service acquisitions reviewed to date.

In 2008, USD(AT&L) incorporated these requirements into DOD Instruction 5000.02, which is part of DOD's overarching policy governing the operation of the defense acquisition system.[14] This instruction currently requires that senior officials across DOD consider a number of factors when reviewing a service acquisition, including

- the source of the requirement,

- the previous approach to satisfying the requirement,

- the total cost of the acquisition,

- the competition strategy, and

- the source selection planning.

USD(AT&L) expects to issue a stand-alone instruction in 2014 for service acquisition policy to replace Enclosure 9 of DOD Instruction 5000.02. Additionally, in a February 2009 memorandum, USD(AT&L) refined its guidance on conducting service acquisition strategy reviews. Specifically, USD(AT&L)'s memorandum identified criteria that service acquisitions must adhere to and that reviewers are to assess, such as use of appropriate contract type, maximization of competition, and inclusion of objective criteria to measure contractor performance.

DOD also established new senior-level management positions, in part, to address legislative requirements, although some roles and responsibilities are still being defined. For example, the 2006 amendment to 10 U.S.C. § 2330 required that USD(AT&L) and the military departments establish commodity managers to coordinate procurement of key categories of services. In 2010 and 2012, USD(AT&L) revised how it organized its contracted services under nine key categories. These categories of

---

[14]Department of Defense Instruction 5000.02, *Operation of the Defense Acquisition System* Encl. 9 (Dec. 8, 2008).

services, referred to as portfolio groups, are (1) research and development, (2) knowledge based, (3) logistics management, (4) electronic and communication, (5) equipment related, (6) medical, (7) facility related, (8) construction, and (9) transportation. In 2011, the military departments began establishing commodity manager positions to improve coordination and assist requiring activities with their procurement of services within these portfolio groups.[15] By July 1, 2013, USD(AT&L) expects to establish similar positions responsible for supporting the DOD-wide procurement of services, but their authorities and responsibilities are not yet fully defined. Additionally, as part of its Better Buying Power Initiative, USD(AT&L) assigned the Principal Deputy Under Secretary of Defense for Acquisition, Technology, and Logistics as DOD's senior manager for service acquisition, responsible for policy, training, and oversight across DOD. Table 1 summarizes the established positions and accompanying responsibilities in descending order of their hierarchy within DOD.

[15]The military departments have different names for the commodity managers, including portfolio managers, program directors, and portfolio coordinators.

Table 1: Description of DOD Positions Responsible for Service Acquisition and Management

Position	Description
Under Secretary of Defense for Acquisition, Technology, and Logistics (USD(AT&L))	• 10 U.S.C. § 2330 requires USD(AT&L) to develop and maintain policies, procedures, and best practices guidelines addressing procurement of contracted services • Senior official for management of service acquisition across DOD • Delegates approval authority for service acquisitions valued at $1 billion or more to the Director of Defense Procurement and Acquisition Policy
Principal Deputy Under Secretary for Acquisition, Technology, and Logistics	• USD(AT&L) designated this position as the senior manager for service acquisition through its April 2013 Better Buying Power Initiative memorandum • While USD(AT&L) is defining specific responsibilities and authorities, DOD officials indicated this position will be generally responsible for policy, training, and oversight of service acquisition across DOD
Director, Defense Procurement and Acquisition Policy	• Responsible for acquisition policy, oversight of Defense Federal Acquisition Regulation Supplement, and other duties within USD(AT&L) • Approval authority for service acquisitions valued at $1 billion or more, as delegated by USD(AT&L)
Military Department Service Acquisition Executives[a]	• 10 U.S.C. § 2330 designated the Service Acquisition Executives as the senior officials responsible for service acquisition in the military departments • Responsible for management, oversight, and departmental policy for service acquisition • Approval authority for service acquisitions valued between $250 million and $1 billion, unless otherwise delegated within their departments
Military Department Senior Services Managers	• USD(AT&L) required the military departments to establish these positions in its September 2010 Better Buying Power Initiative memorandum • Senior manager within the military departments responsible for strategic planning, execution, and management of services within each military department • Approval authority for service acquisitions valued between $10 million and $250 million, unless otherwise delegated within their departments
Military Department Commodity Managers	• 10 U.S.C. § 2330 required these positions be established, but the military departments did not begin creating these positions until 2011 • Service acquisition professionals within the military departments' offices of the senior services managers responsible for coordination of service acquisitions within their assigned portfolio group • Support spend analysis and strategic sourcing efforts within their respective military departments[b] • Not an approval authority for service acquisitions

Source: GAO analysis of DOD data.

[a]Service acquisition executives are responsible for overseeing the acquisition of both products and services within their respective military departments.

[b]Spend analysis provides knowledge about how much is being spent for goods and services, who the buyers are, who the suppliers are, and where the opportunities are to save money and improve performance. Strategic sourcing is defined by the Office of Management and Budget as a structured process based on spend analysis to make business decisions about acquiring commodities and services more efficiently and effectively.

While these positions have a role in reviewing, approving, or coordinating individual service acquisitions, senior USD(AT&L) and military department officials explained that they do not have responsibility or authority for making departmentwide decisions, such as determining current or future resources allocated to contracted services. These officials explained that the military departments' commands and requiring activities are responsible for determining their requirements and how best to meet them, as well as requesting and allocating budgetary resources. For example, while USD(AT&L) officials and the military department senior services managers are responsible for reviewing service acquisitions to determine whether the planned acquisition strategy clearly defines the military department's requirement, they do not determine what contracted services are needed or whether an alternative acquisition approach could better meet their need. USD(AT&L) officials and the military department senior services managers stated they do not have insight into each requiring activity's specific needs and are not positioned to validate those needs.

For additional details on the actions that USD(AT&L) and the military departments have taken to address the specific requirements of 10 U.S.C. § 2330, see appendix I.

DOD Continues to Focus on Improving the Requirements Development Process and Training for Individual Service Acquisitions

USD(AT&L) has planned and implemented actions to improve DOD's process for developing requirements for individual service acquisitions, as required by the 2006 amendment to 10 U.S.C. § 2330.[16] USD(AT&L) officials noted that it has collaborated with DAU officials to develop new tools and training to help DOD personnel develop better acquisitions. For example,

- USD(AT&L) collaborated with DAU to create the Acquisition Requirements Roadmap Tool (ARRT) in 2012. The ARRT is an online resource designed to help personnel write performance-based requirements and create several pre-award documents, including performance work statements and quality assurance surveillance plans. The ARRT guides users through a series of questions to develop the pre-award documents using a standardized template tailored to the specific requirement for services. Although using the

---

[16]Requirements development is the process by which DOD personnel identify a need for a service and translate that need into certain contracting documents, including a performance work statement or quality assurance surveillance plan.

ARRT is not required across DOD, DAU officials told us they have integrated its use into other DAU training, such as the Performance Requirements for Service Acquisitions course. DAU officials did not have data on the effectiveness of the ARRT but noted that feedback has been positive. For example, they have heard that performance work statements are better reflecting requirements as a result of personnel using the tool.

- In 2009, DAU introduced its Services Acquisition Workshop (SAW) to provide training and guidance on developing service acquisition requirements. The SAW is a 4-day workshop tailored to proposed service acquisitions. Upon request from commands or requiring activities, DAU officials travel to the requestor and convene the multifunctional team responsible for an acquisition, including general counsel, individuals associated with the acquisition requirements, contracting personnel, and oversight personnel. This team is then to develop the language that will be used to articulate the service requirement using the ARRT. By the end of the 4 days, the command is to have drafts of its performance work statement, quality assurance surveillance plan, and performance requirement summary. A key aspect of the workshop DAU officials identified is that it brings together the key personnel responsible for the acquisition to discuss the service requirements and how they will know if a contractor has met those requirements. From fiscal years 2009 through 2012, DAU conducted 78 SAWs. In 2012, USD(AT&L) mandated use of the SAW for service acquisitions valued at $1 billion and above and is encouraging its use for acquisitions valued at $100 million or more. USD(AT&L) has directed the Director of Defense Procurement and Acquisition Policy (DPAP) and the senior services managers to assess the effectiveness of the SAW and develop lessons learned and best practices by October 1, 2013.

In addition to implementing the ARRT and the SAW, USD(AT&L) established the Acquisition of Services Functional Integrated Product Team (Services FIPT) in August 2012, in part, to address training requirements in 10 U.S.C. § 2330. According to its charter, the Services FIPT is comprised of the Director of DPAP, DAU officials, and other officials responsible for acquisition career management within the DOD. The Services FIPT is to provide input toward the development and dissemination of training products and practical tools to assist personnel responsible for acquiring services. In addition, the Services FIPT is to explore the feasibility of certification standards and career development for all personnel who acquire services, including personnel within and outside of the defense acquisition workforce. USD(AT&L) officials explained that non-acquisition personnel are most often involved in the requirements development portion of the acquisition process but may not be trained on how DOD buys services. In 2011, we found that non-acquisition personnel with acquisition-related responsibilities represented more than half of the 430 personnel involved in the 29 services contracts we reviewed.[17] While we found that non-acquisition personnel received some acquisition training, this training was largely related to contract oversight as opposed to requirements development. According to its charter, one of the Services FIPT's first tasks will be to identify DOD's non-acquisition personnel involved in service acquisitions and determine how best to train them.

The Services FIPT, however, has made little progress to date, and has met once since it was established. USD(AT&L) officials could not provide a time line for when the Services FIPT may fully address the training requirements in 10 U.S.C. § 2330. The officials explained that they expect the team to make more progress in 2013 when the Principal Deputy Under Secretary for Acquisition, Technology, and Logistics assumes leadership of the Services FIPT.

USD(AT&L) Did Not Develop a Plan to Meet the Requirement of Section 807 but Has Taken Actions to Address Each Element in the Law

Section 807 of the NDAA for Fiscal Year 2012 required USD(AT&L) to develop a plan by June 28, 2012, for implementing the recommendations of the DSB to include, to the extent USD(AT&L) deemed appropriate, the following eight elements:

1. incentives to services contractors for high performance at low cost,

2. communication between the government and the services contracting industry while developing requirements for services contracts,

3. guidance for defense acquisition personnel on the use of appropriate contract types,

4. formal certification and training requirements for services acquisition personnel,

5. recruiting and training of services acquisition personnel,

---

[17]GAO, *Defense Acquisition Workforce: Better Identification, Development, and Oversight Needed for Personnel Involved in Acquiring Services*, GAO-11-892 (Washington, D.C.: Sept. 26, 2011).

6. policies and guidance on career development for services acquisition personnel,

7. ensuring the military departments dedicate portfolio-specific commodity managers, and

8. ensuring DOD conducts realistic exercises and training that account for services contracting during contingency operations.

USD(AT&L) officials told us they did not develop a specific plan to address the section 807 requirement. They explained, however, that the April 2013 Better Buying Power Initiative memorandum addresses seven of the eight elements and that they have addressed the last element through a separate effort. In reviewing the April 2013 memorandum, we also found that it reflects actions to address all of the elements except the one pertaining to training and exercises during contingency operations. USD(AT&L) also identified 23 different actions it has taken or plans to take that officials regard as addressing all of the elements the plan was to include, some of which pre-date the April 2013 Better Buying Power Initiative memorandum. For example,

- In January 2012, USD(AT&L) issued guidance to improve how DOD communicates with the vendor community.

- In April 2013, USD(AT&L) directed that new guidance be developed to help acquisition personnel select the appropriate contract type and contractor performance incentives in DOD's service acquisitions.

- DOD plans to conduct a joint mission rehearsal exercise in 2014 that will include training for services contracting during contingency operations.

See appendix II for a more detailed description of the actions USD(AT&L) took to address the section 807 elements.

DOD Has Not Fully Addressed Key Factors to Determine Whether Actions Are Improving Service Acquisition

While DOD has taken a number of actions to address legislative requirements, DOD is not yet positioned to determine what effects its actions have had on improving service acquisition. Specifically, USD(AT&L) has not yet fully addressed two key factors—a desired end state for the future with specific goals and associated metrics that would enable it to assess progress toward achieving those goals and determine whether service acquisition is improving. USD(AT&L) is challenged in addressing these key factors, in part, because it has limited insight into the current status of service acquisition in terms of the volume, type, location, and trends. While they have not established metrics to assess departmentwide progress, USD(AT&L) officials rely on reviews of individual service acquisitions, command level assessments, and feedback from the military departments as means to gauge whether DOD's efforts are contributing to better service acquisitions. DOD has not established aggregated results or trends which could be used to provide a departmentwide perspective on the effects of its actions.

DOD Does Not Have the Information Needed to Define a Desired End State for Its Improvement Efforts

USD(AT&L) and military department leadership have demonstrated a commitment to improving service acquisition, but USD(AT&L) officials stated that they have not defined the desired end state or specific goals its actions were intended to achieve. In our November 2006 report, we found, based on assessments of leading commercial firms, that identifying and communicating a defined end state or specific goals can significantly improve service acquisition.[18] This work also found that being able to define a desired end state or what goals are to be achieved at a specified time necessitates knowledge of the current volume, type, location, and trends of service acquisitions.

USD(AT&L) and the military department senior services managers acknowledge that they are challenged in defining the desired end state, in part, because limitations within DOD's contracting and financial data systems hinder their insight into where service acquisition is today. USD(AT&L) and military department officials explained that DOD's primary source of information on contracts, the Federal Procurement Data System-Next Generation (FPDS-NG), has a number of data limitations, including that it

---

[18]GAO-07-20.

- only reflects the predominant service purchased on a service contract,

- does not reveal any services embedded in a contract for goods, and

- does not fully identify the location of the requiring activity contracting for the service.

Additionally, DOD's financial systems do not provide detailed information on DOD's budget and actual spending on specific types of contracted services and are not linked to the data maintained in FPDS-NG.[19] According to USD(AT&L) officials and the senior services managers, collectively, the limitations of both FPDS-NG and DOD's financial systems create challenges in identifying the current volume, type, location, and any potential trends in service acquisition. For example, USD(AT&L) stated that DOD wants to more strategically manage its nine portfolio groups of contracted services but does not have adequate insight into what services DOD currently buys within these portfolio groups.

To improve insight into DOD's contracted services, USD(AT&L) is linking DOD's contract and financial data systems and increasing the level of detail these systems provide. For example, DOD is updating its financial systems to provide data on each service purchased under a contract. USD(AT&L) officials stated that improving and linking data within its contract and financial systems will enable DOD to determine what it budgeted for a particular service, what it actually spent for that service, and which organizations bought the service. Officials, however, do not expect to have this capability until at least 2014. USD(AT&L) officials noted that this effort could help provide better insight into future budget requirements for services. USD(AT&L) officials also stated that they are exploring how to use Electronic Document Access—a DOD online document access system for acquisition related information—to provide them with better insight into the different types of services DOD buys under each of its contracts. USD(AT&L) identified that, collectively, these efforts will help them to improve the management of its nine portfolio groups of contracted services, thereby enabling the department to

---

[19]For additional information on DOD's efforts to improve its insight into contracted services, see GAO, *Defense Acquisitions: Continued Management Attention Needed to Enhance Use of DOD's Inventory of Contracted Services,* GAO-13-491 (Washington, D.C.: May 23, 2013).

- better leverage its buying power,

- provide insight into the marketplace and buying behaviors, and

- identify opportunities for cost savings.

In its April 2013 Better Buying Power Initiative memorandum, USD(AT&L) also identified that by managing service acquisition by portfolio group, the senior services managers should be able to work with requiring activities to forecast future services requirements. While the military departments have taken some steps to forecast or track future contracted services requirements, these efforts are too new to determine their utility in identifying what services DOD plans to buy. For example, in 2012, the Army senior services manager requested that Army commands provide an estimate for contracted services valued over $10 million to be purchased over the next five fiscal years in an effort to identify any potential cost savings. Air Force officials also track information on service acquisitions that they expect will be awarded over the next three years to aid in planning acquisition strategy reviews. The Navy is developing its own approach to forecast future contracted services requirements, which officials stated will be implemented in 2013. While it is too early to assess the effects of these forecast or tracking efforts, they have the potential to help the military departments better understand what services will be purchased and facilitate DOD in identifying its desired end state for service acquisition.

USD(AT&L) Has Not Established Metrics to Determine its Progress in Improving Service Acquisition

USD(AT&L) has not established departmentwide metrics to assess the effects of its actions to improve service acquisition. Our prior work found that metrics linked to specified outcomes are another key factor to (1) evaluating and understanding performance levels, (2) identifying critical processes that require attention, (3) documenting results over time, and (4) reporting information to senior officials for decision making purposes.[20] In lieu of such metrics, USD(AT&L) and military department officials stated that they rely on results from reviews of individual service acquisitions, command level assessments, and feedback from the military departments to gauge whether the department's actions to improve services acquisitions, such as those required by Congress or established under DOD's Better Buying Power Initiative, are having a positive effect.

---

[20]GAO-07-20.

USD(AT&L) officials have acknowledged the need to establish departmentwide metrics but explained that developing such metrics has proven challenging. They further indicated that metrics used by leading commercial companies, which often focus on reducing spending for services to improve a company's financial position, may not be appropriate for DOD.[21] USD(AT&L) officials noted that DOD's budget is based on an assessment of its missions and the resources needed to achieve its objective. These officials noted that while DOD is continuously looking for ways to improve its efficiency, it is difficult to set goals and measure actual reductions in spending as any savings or cost avoidances will generally be invested in other unfunded or high priority activities. Further, USD(AT&L) officials noted that since DOD's budget is appropriated by Congress rather than derived from the sale of goods and services, changes in its resources are often outside its direct control.

While developing goals and metrics is challenging, it is not impossible. DOD has acknowledged the need to establish departmentwide metrics. For example, our recent work on strategic sourcing—a process that moves an organization away from numerous individual acquisitions to a broader, aggregate approach—found that federal agencies, including DOD, could expand the use of this approach.[22] Strategic sourcing enables federal agencies to lower costs and maximize the value of services they buy, which is consistent with DOD's Better Buying Power Initiative. We found that some agencies, including DOD, did not address the categories that represented their highest spending, the majority of which exceeded $1 billion and were for services. To improve its strategic sourcing efforts at DOD, we recommended, among other things, that DOD set goals for the amount of spending managed through strategically sourced acquisitions, link strategic sourcing to its Better Buying Power Initiative, and establish metrics, such as utilization rates, to track progress toward these goals. DOD concurred with the recommendations and stated it would establish goals and metrics by September 2013.

In the absence of departmentwide metrics, USD(AT&L) officials and senior services managers identified several ongoing efforts they rely on to

---

[21]For additional information on commercial practices, see GAO, *Strategic Sourcing: Leading Commercial Practices Can Help Federal Agencies Increase Savings When Acquiring Services*, GAO-13-417 (Washington, D.C.: May 15, 2013).

[22]GAO, *Strategic Sourcing: Improved and Expended Use Could Save Billions in Annual Procurement Costs*, GAO-12-919 (Washington, D.C.: Sept. 20, 2012).

GAO-13-634 Defense Acquisitions

gauge the effects of their actions to improve service acquisition. For example, USD(AT&L) and the military departments conduct pre- and post-award independent management reviews, or peer reviews, to ensure individual service acquisitions are conducted in accordance with applicable laws, regulations, and policies.[23] USD(AT&L) and military department officials stated that through these peer reviews, they can determine if individual service acquisitions have resulted in the intended outcomes. For example, during the post-award phase, reviewers are to assess whether cost, schedule, and performance measures associated with individual service acquisitions are being achieved. We have previously found, however, that cost or schedule performance measures may not be as effective for service acquisitions as they are for product or weapon system acquisitions.[24] Further, while peer reviews provide DOD with insight into the performance of a single service acquisition, DOD does not have information on how many post-award peer reviews have been completed by the military departments and has not aggregated the results or identified trends from all of DOD's peer reviews.

Additionally, the Air Force and the Navy are conducting assessments at the command level to evaluate organizations that buy and manage service acquisitions. These assessments are intended to identify performance levels, needed improvements, and best practices. For example, the Air Force implemented health assessments to review a command's timeliness of contract awards, creation and use of standardized templates, implementation of internal and external recommendations and new policy requirements, and quality of communication. According to officials, the Air Force first implemented its health assessments in approximately 2009 to rate or score each of its commands in a number of different performance areas, such as program management and fiscal responsibility. Air Force officials reported, however, that they have not established baselines or identified any quantifiable trends from these health assessments. That said, Air Force officials told us that these assessments have contributed to improvements in the service acquisition process. For example, in a 2011 health assessment, the Air Force found that one program office reduced the use of bridge contracts—a potentially undesirable contract that spans the time between an expiring contract and a new award—by 50 percent from fiscal

---

[23]National Defense Authorization Act for Fiscal year 2007, Pub. L. No. 110-181, § 808 (2008).

[24]GAO-07-20.

year 2010 to 2011.[25] The Navy completed its first health assessment in 2012. During this assessment, the Navy identified a requirements development tool created and used within a command that was potentially a best practice and is being considered for Navy-wide use. The Army's senior services manager is in the process of determining how to assess the health of the Army's service acquisition organizations and expects to implement an approach in 2013.

USD(AT&L) officials also plan to assess the health of service acquisition across the military departments, potentially down to the program office level, using a number of indicators of risks, referred to as tripwires. Tripwires are established thresholds for measurable risk or performance indicators related to the acquisition of goods or services that, when triggered, could result in further review. USD(AT&L) officials stated that tripwires are still under development but could include thresholds for the number of days FPDS-NG data was input past deadlines or the number of contract modifications within 30 days of contract award. USD(AT&L) officials explained that tripwires alone are not sufficient to assess service acquisition performance, but tripwires could provide insight into what may or may not be going well and provide trend data over time.

Further, USD(AT&L) annually reviews the military departments and other DOD components to understand the effects of its actions and policies related to improving service acquisitions and solicit recommendations for changes. For example, in 2012, USD(AT&L) inquired about the actions that have been taken to comply with various defense acquisition regulations or policies, such as the Better Buying Power Initiative. The Army's and Navy's responses noted that actions to improve competition led to an 11 and 12 percent increase, respectively, in the rate of effective competition—situations where more than one offer is received in response to a competitive solicitation—for service contracts from fiscal year 2010 through 2012. In response to an open-ended question on recommendations for improvements, each military department suggested that USD(AT&L) take additional actions to increase departmentwide coordination on service acquisitions. Specifically, the Army and the Air Force recommended departmentwide service acquisition management

---

[25]Our prior work has found that bridge contracts are typically the result of unexpected delays in the acquisition process such as bid protests or undesirable delays due to a lack of sufficient acquisition planning. GAO, *Defense Contracting: Competition for Services and Recent Initiatives to Increase Competitive Procurements*, GAO-12-384 (Washington, D.C.: Mar. 15, 2012).

meetings to coordinate on issues such as emerging regulations, directives, and policies to improve service acquisitions. In response, USD(AT&L) officials told us that the Director of DPAP meets with the military departments' senior services managers regularly.

DOD's ongoing efforts to gauge the effects of their actions to improve service acquisition also offer opportunities for DOD to develop baseline data, establish goals, and identify departmentwide metrics to measure progress. For example, by analyzing and aggregating the results of its health assessments, each military department could establish baselines against which to assess individual commands and over time, identify trends to determine if its commands are improving how they acquire services. Similarly, in coordination with the military departments, USD(AT&L) could use its tripwire approach to determine what percent of DOD's service acquisition strategies are not approved or require changes before approval. DOD could then use such information to help identify reasons for why certain service acquisitions are not approved and determine appropriate corrective actions. DOD could further develop metrics associated with actions outlined in the Better Buying Power Initiative. For example, using its established services portfolio groups, DOD could develop baseline data on the degree of effective competition for services within each group. Depending on the results of that analysis, DOD could determine whether it would be appropriate to establish effective competition goals and metrics for each portfolio group or specific types of services within each group.

Conclusions

In light of the billions of dollars DOD spends each year on services and the constrained fiscal environment, it is critical for DOD to identify how it can best utilize its financial resources and acquire services more efficiently and effectively. DOD leadership has demonstrated a commitment to improving service acquisition and management and has taken a number of actions to address legislative requirements. For example, USD(AT&L) and the military departments have focused more management attention on improving service acquisitions through new policies and guidance, reviews of high-dollar service acquisitions, and new tools and training for personnel who acquire services. Further, DOD recently designated the Principal Deputy Under Secretary of Defense for Acquisition, Technology, and Logistics as the department's senior manager for service acquisition and has established similar positions, including senior services managers, within each of the military departments. In some cases, however, DOD remains in the process of defining the duties and responsibilities of these positions. When taken collectively, DOD has taken action to address the requirements of 10 U.S.C. § 2330 and section 807 of the NDAA for Fiscal Year 2012.

DOD, however, does not know whether or how these actions, individually or collectively, have resulted in improvements to service acquisition. This is due, in part, to the fact that DOD continues to have limited knowledge and baseline data on the current state of service acquisition. To address this shortfall, DOD expects to obtain better service acquisition data by improving and linking data within its contract and financial systems, but this effort will not be complete until at least 2014. Having baseline budget and spending data can provide a foundation for measuring progress, but other factors such as articulating its desired end state and developing specific and measurable goals are also important for assessing progress. While developing specific goals and departmentwide metrics is challenging, it is not impossible. For example, DOD concurred with the need to set goals for the amount of spending managed through strategically sourced acquisitions, link strategic sourcing to its Better Buying Power Initiative, and establish metrics, such as utilization rates, to track progress toward these goals. However, DOD is currently missing opportunities to fully leverage its command-level assessments, feedback from the military departments, and other ongoing efforts it relies on to gauge the effects of its actions to improve service acquisition. Each of these efforts has merit and value in their own regard. Nevertheless, until DOD utilizes them to develop baseline data, goals, and associated metrics, similar to what it has committed to do for its strategic sourcing efforts, DOD will continue to be in a position where it does not know whether its actions are sufficient to achieve desired outcomes.

Recommendations for Executive Action

To better position DOD to determine whether its actions have improved service acquisition, we recommend that the Principal Deputy Under Secretary of Defense for Acquisition, Technology, and Logistics, in consultation with the military departments' senior services managers, take the following three actions:

- identify baseline data on the status of service acquisition, in part, by using budget and spending data and leveraging its ongoing efforts to gauge the effects of its actions to improve service acquisition,

- develop specific goals associated with their actions to improve service acquisition, and

- establish metrics to assess progress in meeting these goals.

Agency Comments and Our Evalutation

DOD provided us with written comments on a draft on this report, which are reprinted in appendix III. DOD concurred with the three recommendations, noting that they are consistent with DOD's ongoing Better Buying Power Initiative. DOD also stated that as it improves its management of service acquisition, it should be able to measure performance, track productivity trends, and establish consistent best practices across the department. We agree that DOD has the opportunity to leverage its ongoing efforts as it works to implement our recommendations. By incorporating our recommendations into those efforts, DOD will be better positioned to determine whether its actions are improving service acquisition. DOD also provided technical comments, which were incorporated as appropriate.

We are sending copies of this report to the Secretary of Defense; the Secretaries of the Army, Air Force, and the Navy; the Principal Deputy Under Secretary of Defense for Acquisition, Technology, and Logistics; and interested congressional committees. This report will also be available at no charge on the GAO website at http://www.gao.gov.

If you or your staff have any questions concerning this report, please contact me at (202) 512-4841 or by e-mail at dinapolit@gao.gov. Contact points for our Offices of Congressional Relations and Public Affairs may be found on the last page of this report. Staff who made key contributions to this report are listed in appendix IV.

Timothy J. DiNapoli
Director
Acquisition and Sourcing Management

List of Committees

The Honorable Carl Levin
Chairman
The Honorable James Inhofe
Ranking Member
Committee on Armed Services
United States Senate

The Honorable Dick Durbin
Chairman
The Honorable Thad Cochran
Ranking Member
Subcommittee on Defense
Committee on Appropriations
United States Senate

The Honorable Howard P. "Buck" McKeon
Chairman
The Honorable Adam Smith
Ranking Member
Committee on Armed Services
House of Representatives

The Honorable C.W. "Bill" Young
Chairman
The Honorable Pete Visclosky
Ranking Member
Subcommittee on Defense
Committee on Appropriations
House of Representatives

Appendix I: Department of Defense Actions to Implement Requirements in 10 U.S.C. § 2330

In 2001, Congress required the Secretary of Defense to implement a management structure for the acquisition of services under section 2330, title 10, United States Code (U.S.C.).[1] This provision requires, among other things, the Department of Defense (DOD) to develop a process for approving individual service acquisitions based on dollar thresholds and other criteria to ensure that DOD acquires services by means that are in the government's best interest and managed in compliance with applicable statutory requirements. Under DOD's initial May 2002 guidance for implementing the required management structure and service acquisition approval process, the Under Secretary of Defense for Acquisition, Technology, and Logistics (USD(AT&L)) was to review all proposed service acquisitions with an estimated value of $2 billion or more. The military departments and other defense components were to review service acquisitions below that threshold.[2] The military departments each subsequently developed their own service acquisition approval processes that had several elements in common. Chief among these elements was the requirement that acquisition strategies be reviewed and approved by senior officials before contracts are awarded. Acquisition strategies to be reviewed were to include, among other things, information on contract requirements, anticipated risks, and business arrangements. Once acquisition strategies were approved, DOD contracting offices may continue the acquisition process, including soliciting bids for proposed work and awarding contracts.

In January 2006, Congress amended 10 U.S.C. § 2330 to include additional requirements for DOD's management of the acquisition of services.[3] The amendment requires, among other things, that the senior officials responsible for management of acquisition of contract services assign responsibility for the review and approval of procurements based on estimated value of the acquisition. Senior officials within DOD are identified as USD(AT&L) and the service acquisition executives of the military departments. In response to these requirements, USD(AT&L) issued an October 2006 memorandum to update its 2002 acquisition of services policy. The revised policy identifies categories of service

---

[1]National Defense Authorization Act for Fiscal Year 2002, Pub. L. No. 107-107, § 801(b) (2001).

[2]Office of the Under Secretary of Defense for Acquisition, Technology, and Logistics, *Acquisition of Services*, May 31, 2002.

[3]National Defense Authorization Act for Fiscal Year 2006, Pub. L. No. 109-163, § 812.

acquisitions, based on dollar thresholds and related roles and responsibilities within USD(AT&L) and the military departments.[4] The policy requires all proposed service acquisitions with a value estimated at more than $1 billion be referred to USD(AT&L) and formally reviewed at the discretion of USD(AT&L).[5] Acquisitions with a value estimated under that threshold are subject to military department acquisition approval reviews.[6] USD(AT&L)'s 2006 acquisition of services policy was incorporated into Enclosure 9 of DOD's 5000.02 acquisition instruction.[7] In 2010, USD(AT&L) required that each of the military departments establish senior managers to be responsible for the governance in planning, execution, strategic sourcing, and management of service contracts. Additionally, these senior managers are to review service acquisitions valued at $10 million but less than $250 million. USD(AT&L) expects to issue a stand-alone instruction in 2014 for service acquisition policy to replace Enclosure 9 of DOD Instruction 5000.02. See table 2 for a summary of service acquisition review thresholds and approval authorities.

[4]Office of the Under Secretary of Defense for Acquisition, Technology, and Logistics, *Acquisition of Services Policy*, October 2, 2006.

[5]The memorandum also provides for the review of "special interest" acquisitions, which are not defined in the memorandum but may be designated as such by USD(AT&L) or other senior officials.

[6]Specifically, under the 2006 policy, a service acquisition valued at greater than the simplified acquisition threshold but not greater than $1 billion by or on behalf of a military department will be reviewed by the senior official responsible for the management of acquisitions of services for the respective military department, or as designated. A service acquisition valued at greater than the simplified acquisition threshold but not greater than $1 billion by or on behalf of the DOD components outside the military departments will be reviewed by the senior official responsible for the management of acquisitions of services for the DOD components, who is USD(AT&L), or as designated.

[7]Although the acquisition of services policy incorporated in enclosure 9 of the 5000.02 instruction is substantially similar to USD(AT&L)'s 2006 policy, the 5000.02 policy provides that for service acquisitions estimated to cost over $1 billion, the senior officials of the military departments and decision authorities in DOD components outside the military departments shall notify USD(AT&L) of the proposed acquisition, and USD(AT&L) or as designated shall initiate a review of the proposed acquisition strategy. The review shall be completed within 30 days and the acquisition may only proceed after the acquisition strategy has been approved. Department of Defense Instruction 5000.02, *Operation of the Defense Acquisition System* Encl. 9, paras. 5.b.(1)-(4).

Table 2: Summary of DOD's Service Acquisition Dollar Thresholds and Approval Authorities

Service acquisition dollar threshold	Approval authority
Any acquisition of services with a total estimated value of $1 billion or more	USD(AT&L) or designee
As designated by USD(AT&L), DOD Chief Information Officer, or military department senior official	USD(AT&L) or senior officials
Acquisitions of services with estimated value of $250 million or more	Military department senior official[a] or as designated
Acquisitions of services with estimated value of $10 million or more, but less than $250 million	Military department senior manager or as designated
Acquisitions of services with estimated value more than the simplified acquisition threshold but less than $10 million	Military department senior manager or as designated

Source: USD(AT&L).

Note: Approval authorities for service acquisitions with an estimated value of under $250 million differ within the military departments, as these responsibilities may be delegated to other officials within each department consistent with USD(AT&L)'s policy. Also, any acquisition of information technology services with a total estimated value greater than $500 million is to be approved by the DOD Chief Information Officer or as designated.

[a]USD(AT&L) is the senior official for other defense agencies with DOD.

The 2006 amendments to 10 U.S.C. § 2330 require DOD to take a number of other actions. For example, DOD is to develop service acquisition policies, guidance, and best practices; appoint full-time commodity managers for key categories of services; and ensure competitive procedures and performance-based contracting be used to the maximum extent practicable. In table 3, we summarize the actions that DOD took in response to the requirements in 10 U.S.C. § 2330. To do so, we collected USD(AT&L) and each military department's self-reported information using a data collection template; corroborated reported actions with related documentation when available; and conducted interviews with knowledgeable agency officials to clarify responses. We did not evaluate the appropriateness or sufficiency of any actions taken or planned by DOD.

Table 3: Actions Identified by USD(AT&L) and Military Departments to Address Requirements in 10 U.S.C. § 2330

10 U.S.C. § 2330 requirements	Actions indentified by USD(AT&L) or the military departments to address requirements
(a) Requirement for management structure. The Secretary of Defense shall establish and implement a management structure for the procurement of contract services for the DOD. The management structure shall provide at a minimum, for the following:	
(a)(1)(A) USD(AT&L) shall develop and maintain (in consultation with the service acquisition executives) policies, procedures, and best practices guidelines addressing procurement of contract services, including policies, procedures, and best practices guidelines for	
(a)(1)(A)(i) acquisition planning;	USD(AT&L) issued DOD Instruction 5000.02 Enclosure 9, "Acquisition of Services," in December 2008. This instruction requires that senior officials or their designees consider various elements in reviewing a planned service acquisition including acquisition planning. The instruction also requires officials to consider the cost of the total acquisition, the availability of funding, opportunities to implement socio-economic business concerns and strategic sourcing, competition strategy, and source selection planning.
	DOD issued its "Guidebook for the Acquisition of Services" in July 2011 to provide guidance for the activities that should be conducted during acquisition planning. The guidance recommends the formation of a multi-functional team to plan and manage an acquisition throughout its lifecycle, a review of current approaches to acquiring the required services, and the need to conduct market research.
	The Office of the Secretary of Defense, Defense Procurement and Acquisition Policy (DPAP) issued, in April 2012, the "Market Research Report Guide For Improving the Tradecraft in Services Acquisition" to aid in the conducting of market research. According to the guidance, it was developed in part to translate DOD's best practices for conducting and documenting market research into standard processes and reports. The guidance includes a template for documenting market research to facilitate more effective collection and sharing of market research across DOD.

10 U.S.C. § 2330 requirements	Actions indentified by USD(AT&L) or the military departments to address requirements
(a)(1)(A)(ii) solicitation and contract award;	USD(AT&L) issued DOD Instruction 5000.02 Enclosure 9, "Acquisition of Services," in December 2008. This instruction requires senior officials or their designees to consider various elements in reviewing a planned service acquisition including the identified approach for solicitation and contract award. Officials are required to consider the type of business arrangement anticipated, pricing arrangements, and proposed evaluation criteria.
	DOD issued its "Guidebook for the Acquisition of Services" in July 2011 to provide guidance for the activities that should be conducted when soliciting and awarding contracts, including factors to consider when determining the type of business arrangement and incentives that will be used. The guidebook also provides instructions for drafting a request for proposal and for performance work statements.
	Defense Acquisition University (DAU) developed the "Acquisition Requirements Roadmap Tool (ARRT)" in 2012 to provide DOD personnel with a step-by-step process for developing performance-based service acquisitions. Among other things, the tool is intended to help users generate a performance work statement tailored to their requirements within a standardized format.
(a)(1)(A)(iii) requirements development and management;	USD(AT&L) issued DOD Instruction 5000.02 Enclosure 9, "Acquisition of Services," in December 2008. This instruction requires that senior officials or their designees consider various elements in reviewing a planned service acquisition including the source of the requirement, outcomes to be achieved, and how the requirement was previously satisfied.
	In 2012, DPAP required the military departments to establish processes for identifying, assessing, reviewing, and validating requirements in response to a separate legislative requirement.[a] The military departments subsequently developed their own processes to meet the requirement.
	DAU developed the ARRT to provide guidance on developing requirements for contractor-provided services. DAU officials told us that, according to ARRT-users, the tool has resulted in more precise language on the requirement for services in performance work statements.
	DAU, in coordination with DPAP, developed the Service Acquisition Workshop in 2009 to provide participants with a tailored, interactive, week-long course on performance-based techniques to service acquisitions. The DPAP-funded workshop sponsors instructors from DAU to travel to commands that are developing new service acquisitions. DAU officials explained that once the workshop is complete, the command will have drafted the performance work statement and quality assurance surveillance plan. DAU reported that it conducted 80 workshops between 2009 and 2012. In December 2012, DPAP issued a policy memorandum requiring that Service Acquisition Workshops be conducted for all service acquisitions valued at $1 billion or more. The memorandum notes that this workshop has improved the quality of requirements documents while increasing the likelihood of competition and shortening acquisition lead times.

10 U.S.C. § 2330 requirements	Actions indentified by USD(AT&L) or the military departments to address requirements
(a)(1)(A)(iv) contract tracking and oversight;	USD(AT&L) issued DOD Instruction 5000.02 Enclosure 9, "Acquisition of Services," in December 2008. This instruction requires that senior officials or their designees consider various elements in reviewing a planned service acquisition including the existing or planned management approach for contract tracking and oversight, and tracking procedures or processes used to monitor contractor performance for the proposed services acquisition.
	DOD Instruction 5000.02 Enclosure 9, "Acquisition of Services," also requires that DOD officials collect service contract data. Officials told us such data is compiled through use of the Federal Procurement Data System-Next Generation (FPDS-NG). USD(AT&L) officials stated that they are taking steps to obtain better service contact budget and expenditure data, in part, due to limitations with FPDS-NG. For example, FPDS-NG data lists a single Product and Service Code, the predominant one purchased, for each contract action rather than detailed information on each type of service purchased under the contract.[b] To improve data on service acquisition, in November 2010, DPAP directed the military departments to organize services spending data into six portfolio groups, which were later increased to nine. USD(AT&L) classified nearly 3,000 different Product and Service Codes within its nine portfolio groups, in part, to enhance its ability to analyze service contract spending and support strategic sourcing initiatives. Additionally, in January 2013, USD(AT&L) began an effort to improve its ability to track service contract budget requests, obligations, and expenditures by requiring the military departments to include Product and Service Code line-item data in both acquisition and financial data systems. USD(AT&L) expects that DOD's data systems will have this capability by October 2013.
	In response to other legislative requirements, DOD components, including the military departments, compile annual inventories of activities performed on their behalf by contractors under contracts for services.[c] The legislation requires DOD to annually compile and review an inventory of activities performed pursuant to contracts to help provide better insights into the number of contractor full-time equivalents providing services to DOD and the functions they are performing. To date, DOD has submitted annual inventories of contracted services for fiscal years 2007 through 2011. GAO, however, has found that DOD inventories have significant limitations and do not accurately reflect the number of contractors providing services to DOD.[d] In response to GAO's recommendations, DOD has identified a number of actions it is taking to more accurately reflect the number of contactors providing services to DOD.

10 U.S.C. § 2330 requirements	Actions indentified by USD(AT&L) or the military departments to address requirements
(a)(1)(A)(v) performance evaluation; and	USD(AT&L) issued DOD Instruction 5000.02 Enclosure 9, "Acquisition of Services," in December 2008. This instruction requires that senior officials or their designees consider various elements in reviewing a planned service acquisition including the plan for evaluating whether the metrics and any other measures identified to guide the acquisition have been achieved; measures shall include the thresholds for cost, schedule, and performance for the acquisition.
	In response to other legislative requirements, USD(AT&L) implemented independent management reviews, commonly referred to as peer reviews, of contracts for services.[e] Peer reviews are conducted by teams composed of senior contracting officials from the military departments and defense agencies as well as legal advisors that are not associated with the service acquisition. Part of the review includes an evaluation of whether the contractor met cost, schedule, and performance requirements. DPAP is responsible for conducting pre- and post-award peer reviews for services acquisitions with an estimated value of $1 billion or more and the military departments, defense agencies, and field activities are responsible for conducting similar reviews for service acquisition under that threshold.
	DOD issued its "Guidebook for the Acquisition of Services" in July 2011 to provide guidance for developing contract performance objectives and metrics, and a methodology for assessing contractor performance. For example, it provides the steps DOD officials should take to develop a quality assurance surveillance plan and ensure that a contracting officer's representative (COR) is appointed and trained to implement that plan.
	DOD issued its "DOD COR Handbook" in March 2012 to provide guidance on the roles and responsibilities of CORs. For example, it provides CORs with guidance on how to perform effective contract quality surveillance as well as supplemental information on COR training requirements.
(a)(1)(A)(vi) risk management;	USD(AT&L) issued DOD Instruction 5000.02 Enclosure 9, "Acquisition of Services," in December 2008. This instruction requires that senior officials or their designees consider various elements in reviewing a planned service acquisition including whether the proposed service acquisition includes an assessment of the current and potential technical, cost, schedule, and performance risks and a plan for mitigating or retiring those risks.
	DOD issued its "Guidebook for the Acquisition of Services" in July 2011 to provide guidance on how to identify, assess, and mitigate cost, schedule, and performance risks.

10 U.S.C. § 2330 requirements	Actions indentified by USD(AT&L) or the military departments to address requirements
(a)(1)(B) USD(AT&L) shall work with the service acquisition executives and other appropriate officials of the DOD -	
(a)(1)(B)(i) to identify the critical skills and competencies needed to carry out the procurement of contract services on behalf of DOD;	In August 2012, USD(AT&L) established an Acquisition of Services Functional Integrated Product Team (Services FIPT), chaired by the director of DPAP, to identify the critical skills, competencies, and training DOD that personnel with service acquisition respons bilities need. According to USD(AT&L) officials, the team has met once since it was established and has not yet determined what these skills and competencies might be. While USD(AT&L) does not have a timeframe for making such decisions, it expects to make more progress in 2013 when the Principal Deputy Under Secretary of Defense for Acquisition, Technology, and Logistics assumes leadership over the team.
(a)(1)(B)(ii) to develop a comprehensive strategy for recruiting, training, and deploying employees to meet the requirements for such skills and competencies; and	USD(AT&L) established the Services FIPT, in part, to identify personnel with service acquisition responsibilities, the critical skills those personnel need to complete their respons bilities and improve service acquisitions, and support a human capital strategy. USD(AT&L) officials explained, as discussed above, that the Services FIPT has not yet developed a comprehensive strategy for recruiting, training, and deploying employees with services acquisition responsibilities.
(a)(1)(B)(iii) to ensure that the military departments and Defense agencies have staff and administrative support that are adequate to effectively perform their duties under this section;	USD(AT&L) issued its April 2013 memorandum "Implementation Directive for Better Buying Power 2.0—Achieving Greater Efficiency and Productivity in Defense Spending." The memorandum identifies a number of actions DOD is taking to improve the professionalism of the total acquisition workforce. These include: (1) establishing higher standards for key leadership positions; (2) establishing increased professional qualification requirements for all acquisition specialties; (3) increasing the recognition and support of excellence in acquisition management; and (4) continuing to increase the cost consciousness of the acquisition workforce. However, the memorandum does not include details on how USD(AT&L) has ensured that the military departments and Defense agencies have staff and administrative support to effectively perform their duties related to the acquisition of services. USD(AT&L) did not identify additional actions to address this requirement.

10 U.S.C. § 2330 requirements	Actions indentified by USD(AT&L) or the military departments to address requirements
(a)(1)(C) USD(AT&L) shall establish contract services acquisition categories, based on dollar thresholds, for the purpose of establishing the level of review, decision authority, and applicable procedures in such categories.	USD(AT&L) issued its October 2006 memorandum, "Acquisitions of Services Policy," in part, to address the requirement to establish a management structure and service acquisition approval process. The policy requires that USD(AT&L) review all proposed service acquisitions valued at over $1 billion or any classified as "special interest." The policy further directed the military departments to issue guidance implementing the policy. USD(AT&L) later implemented pre and post-award peer reviews of services acquisitions in a 2008 policy memorandum responding to requirements in the NDAA for Fiscal Year 2008. While the 2006 and 2008 policy memoranda identified what officials were to consider when reviewing service acquisitions, DPAP issued additional guidance in February 2009. This 2009 guidance establishes key services acquisition tenets including use of a comprehensive acquisition strategy, appropriate contract type, maximum competition, and objective criteria to measure performance. The guidance provides that acquisition strategy reviews and peer reviews will include the extent to which these tenets are demonstrated.
(a)(1)(D) USD(AT&L) shall oversee the implementation of the requirements of this section and the policies, procedures, and best practices guidelines established and developed in response to this section pursuant to subparagraph (A).	USD(AT&L) issued DOD Instruction 5000.02 Enclosure 9, "Acquisition of Services" in December 2008. This instruction requires that senior officials or their designees consider various elements in reviewing a planned service acquisition including whether the proposed service acquisition addresses requirements for acquisition planning, requirements development and management, solicitation and contract award, contract tracking and oversight, performance evaluation, and risk management. The peer review process, which USD(AT&L) also cited as an action to address (a)(1)(A)(v) of this section, is a mechanism to oversee the implementation of the policies, procedures, and best practices guidelines established in response to subparagraph (A). USD(AT&L)'s Services FIPT is part of its efforts to oversee the implementation of the requirements of the policies, procedures, and best practices guidelines established in response to subparagraph (A).

10 U.S.C. § 2330 requirements	Actions indentified by USD(AT&L) or the military departments to address requirements
(b) Duties and respons bilities of senior officials responsible for the management of acquisition of contract services -[	
(b)(1) Except as provided in paragraph 2, the senior officials responsible for the management of acquisition of contract services shall assign respons bility for the review and approval of procurements in each contract services acquisition category established under subsection (a)(1)(C) to specific DOD officials, subject to the direction, supervision, and oversight of such senior officials.	While the USD(AT&L) is the senior official respons ble for the management of acquisition of contract services for and on behalf of the defense agencies and other components outside the military departments, USD(AT&L) assigned the Principal Deputy Under Secretary of Defense for Acquisition, Technology, and Logistics as DOD's senior manager for service acquisition, responsible for policy, training, and oversight across DOD. Officials stated, however, that specific roles and responsibilities with respect to service acquisition are still being defined. USD(AT&L) officials stated that they have selected the individual who will assume this position, but cannot proceed until a DOD hiring freeze is lifted. The military departments established similar positions between 2010 and 2012, known as senior services managers, at the direction of USD(AT&L). These managers are respons ble for the governance in planning, execution, strategic sourcing, and management of service contracts.

Each of the military departments developed a management structure and acquisition strategy review policy to compliment USD(AT&L)'s 2006 policy. For each military department, the service acquisition executive is respons ble for the overall management and acquisition of contract services. The military departments' policies identify contract service acquisition categories and approval respons bilities based, in part, on dollar thresholds. The policies generally require that service acquisitions valued over $1 billion, unless indentified as "special interest," be referred to USD(AT&L) for review and approval. However, for service acquisitions under $1 billion, the thresholds and review responsibilities differ by each military department. For example

• The Air Force requires that any service acquisition valued between $100 million and $1 billion be referred to the Air Force Program Executive Office for Combat and Mission Support.

• Navy officials stated that any service acquisition valued between $100 million and $1 billion be referred to Deputy Assistant Secretary of the Navy for Acquisitions.

• The Army requires that service acquisitions valued between $500 million and $1 billion be referred to Deputy Assistant Secretary of the Army for Procurement.

• While the military departments' senior services managers also support the review of these large dollar services acquisitions, they are also the decision authority for service acquisitions valued at $250 million or less, but can delegate that respons bility.

The military departments delegate decision authority for certain lower dollar services acquisitions to other officials such as the head of contracting authority or base commanders. These authorities are delegated for service acquisitions valued as low as the simplified acquisition threshold, as required by USD(AT&L). |

10 U.S.C. § 2330 requirements	Actions indentified by USD(AT&L) or the military departments to address requirements
(b)(2) With respect to the acquisition of contract services by a component or command of DOD the primary mission of which is the acquisition of products and services, such acquisitions shall be conducted in accordance with policies, procedures, and best practices guidelines developed and maintained by the USD(AT&L) pursuant to subsection (a)(1), subject to oversight by the senior officials referred to in paragraph (1).	USD(AT&L) issued DOD Instruction 5000.02 Enclosure 9, "Acquisition of Services," in December 2008. This instruction requires that all acquisitions of services shall comply with applicable statutes, regulations, policies, and other requirements, whether the services are acquired by or on behalf of DOD. The military departments' service acquisition review processes, oversight by the senior services managers, and other policies or instructions ensure that service acquisitions comply with USD(AT&L) policies, procedures and best practice guidelines. For example • The Army's senior services manager conducts an annual forecast of contract services, assesses costs savings quarterly, reviews service acquisition strategies valued between $10 million and $250 million, and annually reviews command processes for awarding service contracts. • The Navy revises the Navy Marine Corps Acquisition Regulation to incorporate service acquisition policy information where appropriate, annually reviews command procedures for awarding services contracts, and requires that individuals who award contracts ensure compliance with both Navy and USD(AT&L) policies, procedures, and best practices. • The Air Force policies governing service acquisitions require similar compliance. The Air Force also noted that its senior services manager is developing additional instructions to strengthen requirements to increase compliance with USD(AT&L) and other policies, procedures, and best practices.
(b)(3) In carrying out paragraph (1), each senior official responsible for the management of acquisition of contract services shall	
(b)(3)(A) implement the requirements of this section and the policies, procedures, and best practices guidelines developed by the USD(AT&L) pursuant to subsection (a)(1)(A);	USD(AT&L) issued DOD Instruction 5000.02 Enclosure 9, "Acquisition of Services," in December 2008. This instruction requires that all acquisitions of services shall comply with applicable statutes, regulations, policies, and other requirements, whether the services are acquired by or on behalf of DOD. The military departments' management structure and service acquisition review process, reviews of command procedures for awarding services acquisitions, and various policies and procedures implement the requirements of this section, as well as the policies, procedures, and best practices guidelines developed by USD(AT&L) pursuant to section (a)(1)(A).

10 U.S.C. § 2330 requirements	Actions indentified by USD(AT&L) or the military departments to address requirements
(b)(3)(B) authorize the procurement of contract services through contracts entered into by agencies outside DOD in appropriate circumstances, in accordance with the requirements of section 854 of the Ronald W. Reagan NDAA for Fiscal Year 2005 (10 U.S.C. § 2304 note), section 814 of the Strom Thurmond NDAA for Fiscal Year 1999 (31 U.S.C. § 1535 note), and the regulations implementing such sections;	Defense Federal Acquisition Regulation Supplement subpart 217.78 and part 242.002 provide DOD policy on contracts or delivery orders issued by a non-DOD agency, and interagency agreements. Each of the military departments has also issued policies or procedures for procuring services through interagency agreements. For example • Subpart 5117.78 of the Army Federal Acquisition Regulation Supplement provides Army policy and procedures for contracts awarded by other entities, • Subpart 5217.5 of the Navy Marine Corps Acquisition Regulation Supplement provides Navy policy and procedures for interagency agreements, and • Air Force Instruction 65-116 and Mandatory Procedure 5317.5 provides Air Force policy and procedures for entering into interagency agreements.
(b)(3)(C) dedicate full-time commodity managers to coordinate the procurement of key categories of services;	USD(AT&L) issued DOD Instruction 5000.02 Enclosure 9, "Acquisition of Services" in December 2008. This instruction requires that the senior officials dedicate commodity managers to coordinate the procurement of key categories of services. All of the military departments reported that they began to assign such commodity managers in 2012. The commodity managers we met with explained that their roles include providing procurement advice to commands within their military department, tracking service contract spending and forecasting data, and assisting in the evaluation of individual service acquisitions and command procedures for developing, awarding, and managing service acquisitions. Officials noted that these managers are sometimes respons ble for the coordination of more than one service portfolio group. USD(AT&L) officials stated that by July 1, 2013, they will establish commodity managers within their office to support service acquisition across DOD. These officials also stated that the roles and responsibilities of commodity managers across DOD will be further defined in the DOD instruction that will replace Enclosure 9 of DOD Instruction 5000.02 in 2014.
(b)(3)(D) ensure that contract services are procured by means of procurement action that are in the best interests of DOD and are entered into and managed in compliance with applicable laws, regulations, directives, and requirements;	USD(AT&L) and the military departments' management structure and service acquisition review process in combination with a number of policies ensure that contract services are procured in the best interest of the DOD and comply with applicable laws, regulations, directives, and requirements.

10 U.S.C. § 2330 requirements	Actions indentified by USD(AT&L) or the military departments to address requirements
(b)(3)(E) ensure that competitive procedures and performance-based contracting are used to the maximum extent practicable for the procurement of contract services; and	USD(AT&L) issued its October 2006 memorandum "Acquisition of Services Policy" and December 2008 DOD Instruction 5000.02 Enclosure 9, "Acquisition of Services," to require that senior officials ensure that services acquisitions are based on clear, performance-based requirements and that cost, schedule, and performance outcomes are identifiable and measurable.
	USD(AT&L) issued its April 2013 memorandum "Implementation of Better Buying Power 2.0—Achieving Greater Efficiency and Productivity in Defense Spending." Within the memorandum, USD(AT&L) emphasized the need to promote effective competitive procedures across DOD. The memorandum includes a number of actions USD(AT&L) has planned to promote competition, including providing more opportunities for small business participation.
	The military departments' management structure and services acquisition review processes, various policies, and reviews of command process for awarding contracts ensure that competitive procedures and performance-based contracting are used to the maximum extent practicable.
(b)(3)(F) monitor data collection under section 2330a of this title, and periodically conduct spending analyses, to ensure that funds expended for the procurement of contract services are being expended in the most rational and economic manner practicable.	In response to other legislative requirements, DOD components, including the military departments, compile annual inventories of activities performed on their behalf by contractors under contracts for services.[9] The legislation requires DOD to annually compile and review an inventory of activities performed pursuant to contracts to help provide better insights into the number of contractor full-time equivalents providing services to DOD and the functions they are performing. To date, DOD has submitted annual inventories of contracted services for fiscal years 2007 through 2011. GAO, however, has found that DOD inventories have significant limitations and do not accurately reflect the number of contractors providing services to DOD.[h] In response to GAO's recommendations, DOD has identified a number of actions it is taking to more accurately reflect the number of contactors providing services to DOD.
	Each of the military departments also identified that their senior services managers conduct service contract spending analyses that are either in support of or in addition to its inventory of activities performed by contractors.

Source: GAO analysis of DOD data.

[a]Ike Skelton National Defense Authorization Act for Fiscal Year 2011, Pub. L. No. 111-383, § 863.

[b]Product and Service Codes are used within FPDS-NG to identify and classify the services, supplies, and equipment purchased under a contract.

[c]National Defense Authorization Act for Fiscal Year 2008, Pub. L. No. 110-181, § 807.

[d]GAO, Defense Acquisitions: Continued Management Attention Needed to Enhance Use and Review of DOD's Inventory of Contracted Services, GAO-13-491 (Washington, D.C.: May 23, 2013).

[e]National Defense Authorization Act for Fiscal Year 2008, Pub. L. No. 110-181, § 808.

[f]10 U.S.C. § 2330(a)(2) and (3) provide that the senior official responsible for the management of acquisition of contract services is the service acquisition executive with respect to the military departments and USD(AT&L) with respect to the defense agencies and other components of DOD.

[9]National Defense Authorization Act for Fiscal Year 2008, Pub. L. No. 110-181, § 807.

[h]GAO-13-491.

Appendix II: Under Secretary of Defense for Acquisition, Technology, and Logistics Actions to Address Elements in Section 807 of the National Defense Authorization Act for Fiscal Year 2012

Section 802 of the National Defense Authorization Act (NDAA) for Fiscal Year 2010[8] required the Under Secretary of Defense for Acquisition, Technology, and Logistics (USD(AT&L)) to direct the Defense Science Board (DSB) to independently assess improvements to the Department of Defense's (DOD) acquisition and oversight of services.[9] The resulting March 2011 DSB report, "Improvements to Services Contracting," contained 20 recommendations aimed at improving DOD's contracting for services. These recommendations focused on developing new policies and processes to strengthen management and oversight of services contracting, designating roles and leadership responsibilities, and strengthening the skills and capabilities of personnel involved in services contracting, including those in contingency environments. Subsequently, section 807 of the NDAA for Fiscal Year 2012 required USD(AT&L) to develop a plan, by June 28, 2012, to implement the DSB recommendations.[10] The plan was to address, to the extent USD(AT&L) deemed appropriate, eight different elements most of which align with the DSB recommendations.

USD(AT&L) officials told us they did not develop a specific plan to address the section 807 requirement, but that the April 2013 Better Buying Power Initiative memorandum addresses seven of the eight elements. In reviewing the memorandum, we also found that it reflects actions to address all of the elements except the one pertaining to training and exercises during contingency operations. USD(AT&L) also identified 23 different actions it has taken or plans to take that officials regard as addressing all of the elements the plan was to include, a number which pre-date the April 2013 Better Buying Power Initiative memorandum.

---

[8]Pub. L. No. 111-84, § 802 (2009).

[9]The DSB is a federal advisory committee established to provide independent advice and recommendations on science, technology, manufacturing, acquisition process, and other matters of special interest to the Secretary of Defense.

[10]Pub. L. No. 112-81, § 807 (2011).

GAO-13-634 Defense Acquisitions

Appendix II: Under Secretary of Defense for
Acquisition, Technology, and Logistics
Actions to Address Elements in Section 807 of
the National Defense Authorization Act for
Fiscal Year 2012

Table 4 provides a summary of the actions USD(AT&L) reported as addressing each of the eight section 807 elements. To determine if USD(AT&L) has taken or planned actions to address the elements in section 807, we collected USD(AT&L)'s self-reported information using a data collection template, corroborated reported actions with related documentation when available, and conducted interviews with knowledgeable USD(AT&L), military department, and Defense Acquisition University officials to clarify responses. We did not evaluate the appropriateness or sufficiency of any actions taken or planned by USD(AT&L).

Appendix II: Under Secretary of Defense for
Acquisition, Technology, and Logistics
Actions to Address Elements in Section 807 of
the National Defense Authorization Act for
Fiscal Year 2012

Table 4: Summary of USD(AT&L)-Identified Actions that Address Elements of Section 807 of the NDAA for Fiscal Year 2012

Element of section 807 of the NDAA for Fiscal Year 2012	Actions identified by USD(AT&L)
1. Meaningful incentives to services contractors for high performance at low cost, consistent with the objectives of the Better Buying Power Initiative established by the Under Secretary. *Note: Text in italics explains Better Buying Power Initiative objectives.*	*USD(AT&L) established its Better Buying Power Initiative in September 2010 with its memorandum, "Better Buying Power: Guidance for Obtaining Greater Efficiency and Productivity in Defense Spending." One of the Better Buying Power Initiative focus areas is "incentivize productivity and innovation in industry." The area includes five principle actions that focus on the tie between profit and performance, contract type justification, the use of progress payments, a preferred supplier program, and independent research and development.* USD(AT&L)'s October 2006 "Acquisitions of Services Policy" memorandum established its process for reviewing and approving service acquisitions and requires senior officials or their designees to consider various elements in reviewing a service acquisition strategy.[a] USD(AT&L) issued additional guidance in February 2009 that established key services acquisition tenets and required that acquisition strategy reviews document the extent to which these key tenets are demonstrated. One of these tenets is that the service acquisitions include objective incentives, whenever possible. The guidance also provides instruction for how reviewers are to assess the use of such incentives. In December 2012, USD(AT&L) required that DOD personnel developing service acquisitions with an estimated value of $1 billion or more participate in Defense Acquisition University's (DAU) Services Acquisition Workshop. The workshop is a four-day, team-based training tailored to individual proposed service acquisitions to help develop contractor performance incentives. Through the workshop, DOD personnel use the Acquisition Requirements Roadmap Tool (ARRT) to develop their service acquisition requirement. This tool is an online resource designed to help acquisition personnel write performance-based requirements for service acquisitions and draft several pre-award documents. According to USD(AT&L) officials, the ARRT helps personnel articulate desired service acquisition outcomes, which helps them to develop contractor performance incentives. USD(AT&L) officials stated that as leadership within the military departments participate in the Services Acquisition Workshops and are exposed to the use of the ARRT, the use of this tool will become institutionalized throughout DOD. In response to other legislative requirements, USD(AT&L) hosted a public meeting in March 2013 to obtain the views of experts and interested parties in government and the private sector regarding the profit guidelines in the Defense Federal Acquisition Regulation Supplement.[b] This meeting was to help USD(AT&L) revise DOD profit policy guidelines and to identify any modifications to such guidelines that are necessary to ensure an appropriate link between contractor profit and contractor performance. According to USD(AT&L) officials, any changes to DOD profit policy will affect contracting incentives. In April 2013, USD(AT&L) updated the Better Buying Power Initiative with a memorandum entitled, "Implementation Directive for Better Buying Power 2.0 – Achieving Greater Efficiency and Productivity in Defense Spending." USD(AT&L), through this initiative, identified the need for incentivizing productivity and innovation in industry and government to achieve its goal of greater efficiency and productivity in defense spending. The memorandum specifies a number of actions DOD plans to take to improve the use of incentives in its acquisitions, including those for services. USD(AT&L) officials identified that one of the memorandum's actions is to provide additional guidance on the use of incentives by updating the 1969 "DOD and National Aeronautics and Space Administration Incentive Contracting Guide."[c] According to the memorandum, a draft of the revised guidance is due by July 1, 2013.

Appendix II: Under Secretary of Defense for
Acquisition, Technology, and Logistics
Actions to Address Elements in Section 807 of
the National Defense Authorization Act for
Fiscal Year 2012

Element of section 807 of the NDAA for Fiscal Year 2012	Actions identified by USD(AT&L)
2. Improved means of communication between the government and the services contracting industry in the process of developing requirements for services contracts.	USD(AT&L) issued a January 2012 "Vendor Communication Plan," noting its commitment to engaging in timely, constructive, and professional information exchanges with the vendor community. It noted specific actions it would take, including the publication of industry engagement opportunities, outreach to small businesses, and holding pre-solicitation conferences.
	USD(AT&L) issued its April 2012 "Market Research Report Guide for Improving The Tradecraft in Services Acquisition," to aid contracting personnel in conducting market research. According to the guidance, it was developed, in part, to translate DOD's best practices for conducting and documenting market research into standard processes and reports. The guidance includes a template for documenting market research to provide for more effective collection and sharing of market research across DOD. According to USD(AT&L) officials, the guide helps acquisition personnel solicit better information when conducting market research and interacting with the contracting community.
	In December 2012, Defense Procurement and Acquisition Policy (DPAP) issued a policy memorandum requiring that Services Acquisition Workshops be conducted for all service acquisitions valued at $1 billion or more, noting that this workshop has improved the quality of requirements documents while increasing the likelihood of competition, and shortening acquisition lead times. In its April 2013 Better Buying Power Initiative memorandum, USD(AT&L) directed the Director of DPAP and the senior services managers to assess the effectiveness of the Services Acquisition Workshop and develop lessons learned and best practices by October 1, 2013. According to USD(AT&L) officials, improving requirements definition will also promote better communication with the services contracting industry as contract solicitation documents will more clearly articulate DOD's needs.
3. Clear guidance for defense acquisition personnel on the use of appropriate contract types for particular categories of services contracts.	USD(AT&L)'s February 2009 memorandum "Review Criteria for the Acquisition of Services" established key services acquisition tenets and requires that acquisition strategy reviews include the extent to which these key tenets are demonstrated. One of these tenets is that service acquisitions include the appropriate contract type.
	USD(AT&L) issued a class deviation from Federal Acquisition Regulation section16.601(d)(1) and Defense Federal Acquisition Regulation Supplement sections 216.601(d)(i) and (ii), regarding limitations on the use of labor hour and time and materials contract types in October 2012. The class deviation adds additional requirements for a determination and finding supporting the use of these contract types. The class deviation does not, however, direct the usage of certain contract types for particular categories of services.
	In accordance with USD(AT&L)'s April 2013 update to the Better Buying Power Initiative, the Director of Defense Pricing is developing guidance on the appropriate use of contract types that will include examples of when to use specific contract types in developing service acquisitions. According to the April 2013 Better Buying Power Initiative memorandum, this guidance will encourage acquisition officials to consider the full range of contract types before deciding on an acquisition approach, although the USD(AT&L) continues to emphasize the use of fixed-price incentive contracts in certain situations.[d] The memorandum further notes that the use of a specific contract type should be governed by the nature of the work and deliverables being placed on contract.

Appendix II: Under Secretary of Defense for
Acquisition, Technology, and Logistics
Actions to Address Elements in Section 807 of
the National Defense Authorization Act for
Fiscal Year 2012

Element of section 807 of the NDAA for Fiscal Year 2012	Actions identified by USD(AT&L)
4. Formal certification and training requirements for service acquisition personnel, consistent with the requirements of sections 1723 and 1724 of title 10 United States Code (U.S.C.). *Note: Text in italics explains sections 1723 and 1724 of title 10, U.S.C.*	*Section 1723, title 10 U.S.C., requires that the Secretary of Defense establish education, training and experience requirements for each acquisition position or category of acquisition positions, except, pursuant to §1733, for critical positions. It also requires, for each career path, that the Secretary of Defense, acting through USD(AT&L), establish requirements for completion of course work and on-the-job training and demonstration of qualifications. Section 1724, title 10 U.S.C., provides that the Secretary of Defense: shall require completion of courses, two years of experience in a contracting position, and a baccalaureate degree to qualify for a contracting officer position, with authority to award or administer contracts for amounts above the simplified acquisition threshold; shall require a baccalaureate to qualify for a GS-1102 position and similar military position; may establish developmental programs; and shall establish qualifications for the contingency contracting force.* In August 2012, USD(AT&L) established an Acquisition of Services Functional Integrated Product Team (Services FIPT), currently chaired by the Director of DPAP, to determine the certification and training requirements for DOD's acquisition personnel. The Services FIPT is responsible for identifying the critical skills, competencies, and training DOD personnel with service acquisition responsibilities need. According to USD(AT&L) officials, while the team has met once since it was established, it has not yet determined formal certification and training requirements related to services acquisitions. USD(AT&L) officials could not provide a timeline for when the Services FIPT may fully address such requirements, but officials stated they are gathering information needed to make their decisions. Further, in April 2013, USD(AT&L) updated the Better Buying Power Initiative and identified the Services FIPT as a means to develop training solutions that address the needs of those responsible for managing service acquisitions. USD(AT&L) officials explained that DOD's acquisition workforce includes individuals who buy both products and services and they have no current plans to develop a separate career path for personnel acquiring services. According to USD(AT&L) officials, senior officials responsible for service acquisitions across DOD are planning to meet with the Services FIPT to discuss what policies and guidance may be needed for acquisition career development in fiscal years 2014 through 2018. While USD(AT&L) has not determined specific training requirements for personnel acquiring services, the Defense Acquisition University (DAU) has developed a number of different service acquisition-related classroom courses and online training materials and guidance that are open to all DOD personnel. In addition, DAU provides online resources for personnel conducting service acquisitions, such as the ARRT.

GAO-13-634 Defense Acquisitions

Appendix II: Under Secretary of Defense for
Acquisition, Technology, and Logistics
Actions to Address Elements in Section 807 of
the National Defense Authorization Act for
Fiscal Year 2012

Element of section 807 of the NDAA for Fiscal Year 2012	Actions identified by USD(AT&L)
5. Appropriate emphasis on the recruiting and training of services acquisition personnel, consistent with the strategic workforce plan developed pursuant to section 115b of title 10 U.S.C. and the funds available through the Department of Defense Acquisition Workforce Development Fund (DAWDF), established pursuant to section 1705 of title 10, U.S.C. *Note: Text in italics explains sections 115b and 1705 of title 10, U.S.C.*	*Section 115b, title 10, U.S.C., requires the Secretary of Defense to submit a strategic workforce plan in every even-numbered year to shape and improve DOD's civilian workforce. The Under Secretary of Defense for Personnel & Readiness shall have overall responsibility for developing and implementing the strategic workforce plan in consultation with USD(AT&L).[e] Section 1705, title 10, U.S.C., requires the Secretary of Defense to establish DAWDF to provide funds, in addition to other funds that may be available, for the recruitment, training, and retention of acquisition personnel. This section establishes rules concerning the use and transfer of DAWDF funds and identifies USD(AT&L), acting through the senior official designated to manage the fund, as the source of guidance for the administration of the fund.[f]* In August 2012, USD(AT&L) established its Services FIPT to determine the training and recruitment requirements for DOD service acquisition personnel. The August 2012 charter outlining the Service FIPT roles and responsibilities identified that the team is responsible for identifying the critical skills, competencies, and training DOD personnel with service acquisition responsibilities need, including but not limited to acquisition personnel. The charter also identifies recruitment and retention of service acquisition personnel as an area the Services FIPT is to address. According to USD(AT&L) officials, the team has met only once since it was established and has not yet determined how it will emphasize recruitment and training for personnel with service acquisition responsibilities or how this effort will be consistent with the strategic workforce plan. USD(AT&L) officials could not provide a timeline for when the Services FIPT may fully address training and recruitment, but stated they are gathering information needed to make their decisions. Further, in April 2013, USD(AT&L) updated the Better Buying Power Initiative and identified the Services FIPT as a means to develop training solutions that address the needs of those responsible for managing service acquisitions. USD(AT&L) officials reported they have taken actions to support acquisition personnel and have worked with DAU to make changes to its acquisition workforce curriculum.

Appendix II: Under Secretary of Defense for
Acquisition, Technology, and Logistics
Actions to Address Elements in Section 807 of
the National Defense Authorization Act for
Fiscal Year 2012

Element of section 807 of the NDAA for Fiscal Year 2012	Actions identified by USD(AT&L)
6. Policies and guidance on career development for service acquisition personnel, consistent with the requirements of section 1722a and 1722b of title 10 U.S.C. *Note: Text in italics explains sections 1722a and 1722b of title 10, U.S.C.*	*Section 1722a provides that the Secretary of Defense shall require the secretary of each military department and USD(AT&L) to establish policies and guidance to ensure development, assignment, and employment of members of the armed forces in the acquisition field.*[9] *Section 1722b provides that the Secretary of Defense, acting through the USD(AT&L), shall establish policies and guidance to ensure development, assignment, and employment of civilian members of the acquisition workforce.*[h] In August 2012, USD(AT&L) established its Services FIPT to determine career development requirements for DOD service acquisition personnel. The August 2012 charter outlining the Services FIPT roles and responsibilities identified that the team is responsible for providing information, perspectives, and recommendations to guide decisions on career development for the service acquisition workforce. USD(AT&L) officials explained that DOD's acquisition workforce includes individuals who buy both products and services and they have no plans to develop a separate career path for personnel acquiring services. According to USD(AT&L) officials, senior managers responsble for service acquisition within the military departments and the Services FIPT are planning to meet to discuss policies and guidance for acquisition career development, specifically identifying priorities for fiscal years 2014 through 2018. Officials emphasized that DOD does not distinguish between personnel acquiring services or systems, and has no plans to establish a separate career path for the acquisition of services. In April 2013, USD(AT&L) updated the Better Buying Power Initiative with a memorandum entitled, "Implementation Directive for Better Buying Power 2.0 – Achieving Greater Efficiency and Productivity in Defense Spending." USD(AT&L), through this initiative, identified the need for qualification standards for acquisition personnel in leadership positions for all types of acquisitions, including services. USD(AT&L) will establish qualification boards to certify DOD acquisition personnel as qualified for key leadership positions. According to the memorandum, board certification is expected to be a factor in promotion.

Appendix II: Under Secretary of Defense for
Acquisition, Technology, and Logistics
Actions to Address Elements in Section 807 of
the National Defense Authorization Act for
Fiscal Year 2012

Element of section 807 of the NDAA for Fiscal Year 2012	Actions identified by USD(AT&L)
7. Actions to ensure that the military departments dedicate portfolio-specific commodity managers to coordinate the procurement of key categories of contract services, as required by section 2330(b)(3)(C) of title 10 U.S.C. *Note: Text in italics explains section 2330(b)(3)(C) of title 10 U.S.C.*	*Section 2330(b)(3)(C), title 10 U.S.C., requires that the senior officials responsible for the management and acquisition of contract services dedicate full-time commodity managers to coordinate the procurement of key categories of services.[i]* USD(AT&L) issued DOD Instruction 5000.02 Enclosure 9, "Acquisition of Services," in December 2008. This instruction requires senior officials to determine key categories of services for DOD and dedicate full-time commodity mangers to coordinate procurement of these services.[j] The military departments began to establish commodity manager positions in 2011 to help coordinate the procurement of services portfolio groups. Army, Navy, and Air Force commodity mangers explained that their roles include providing procurement advice to commands within their military department, collection of service contract spending and forecasting data, and assistance in the evaluation of individual service acquisitions and command procedures for developing, awarding, and managing service acquisitions. USD(AT&L) officials told us that they anticipate establishing DOD-wide commodity manager positions within its office, but officials did not have further details or a time frame for when such positions may be established. USD(AT&L) issued its September 2010 memorandum "Better Buying Power: Guidance for Obtaining Greater Efficiency and Productivity in Defense Spending." The memorandum established six key categories of spending on services, also known as portfolio groups. USD(AT&L) revised these portfolios from six to nine in 2012. The nine portfolios are (1) research and development, (2) knowledge-based, (3) logistics management, (4) electronic and communication, (5) equipment related, (6) medical, (7) facility related, (8) construction, and (9) transportation services. In its April 2013 memorandum to update the Better Buying Power Initiative, USD(AT&L) required that each senior services manager, including those within the military departments, appoint commodity managers for each of these portfolio groups by July 1, 2013. USD(AT&L) expects to issue a stand-alone instruction in 2014 for service acquisition policy to replace Enclosure 9 of DOD Instruction 5000.02. Officials stated that the new instruction will include more specific language on the roles and respons bilities of the commodity managers.

GAO-13-634 Defense Acquisitions

Element of section 807 of the NDAA for Fiscal Year 2012	Actions identified by USD(AT&L)
8. Actions to ensure that DOD conducts realistic exercises and training that account for services contracting during contingency operations, as required by section 2333(e) of title 10 U.S.C. *Note: Text in italics explains section 2333(e) of title 10 U.S.C.*	*Section 2333(e), title 10 U.S.C., requires that the joint policy for requirements definition, contingency program management, and contingency contracting required by section 2333(a) provide for training of military personnel outside the acquisition workforce who are expected to have acquisition responsibility during combat operations, post-conflict operations, and contingency operations. The joint policy shall also provide for the incorporation of contractors and contract operations in mission readiness exercises for operations that will include contracting and contractor support.[k]* USD(AT&L)'s Contingency Contracting Handbook, updated in October 2012, provides tools, templates, and training that enable a contingency contracting officer to be effective in any contracting environment. While the handbook does not provide guidance specifically to military personnel outside the acquisition workforce, USD(AT&L) officials explained that such personnel use the handbook as a reference document. In addition, according to USD(AT&L) officials, DOD provides tools to assist non-acquisition personnel in contingency environments, such as the Contingency Acquisition Support Model for Requirements Generation and the Contingency Contracting Officer's Representative Handbook. The Contingency Acquisition Support Model is a web-based application designed to assist those individuals responsible for initiating contacting requirements in a contingency environment. The application identifies the documents required to initiate a contract, provides templates for the documents, and routes the documents to the appropriate reviewers and approvers. The Contingency Contracting Officer's Representative Handbook provides guidance for personnel acting as Contracting Officer's Representatives in a contingency environment. DOD plans to conduct a joint mission rehearsal exercise in 2014 that will include training for contracting during contingency operations. According to a Joint Staff briefing, this exercise builds on a model the Army Contracting Command established in its "Operation Joint Dawn" exercises in 2011 and 2012 that provided contingency contracting training to deployable military and civilian contracting officers. USD(AT&L) officials confirmed that this exercise will include non-acquisition personnel. According to USD(AT&L) officials, contingency contracting training is also being integrated into education provided by the National Defense University and Army Staff College. These officials stated that non-acquisition personnel would be among the training recipients.

Source: GAO analysis of DOD documents.

[a]USD(AT&L) established its 2006 "Acquisition of Services Policy" memorandum to address the requirement under 10 U.S.C. § 2330 that it develop a management structure for the procurement of contract services. This policy requires that all proposed service acquisitions with an estimated total value of over $1 billion be referred to USD(AT&L) and formally reviewed at USD(AT&L)'s discretion. The military departments are responsble for reviewing acquisitions valued below this threshold. See Appendix II for more information on USD(AT&L)'s actions to address the requirements of 10 U.S.C. § 2330.

[b]National Defense Authorization Act for Fiscal Year 2013, Pub. L. No. 112-239, § 804.

[c]Department of Defense and National Aeronautics and Space Administration, Incentive Contracting Guide, October 1969.

[d]A fixed-price incentive contract is a contract that allows for the adjusting of profit and establishing the final contract price by application of a formula based on the relationship of the total final negotiated cost to the total target cost. The final price is subject to a price ceiling, negotiated at the outset. Federal Acquisition Regulation § 16.403.

[e]10 U.S.C. § 115b(a).

[f]10 U.S.C. § 1705.

[g]10 U.S.C. § 1722a(a).

[h]10 U.S.C. § 1722b(a).

[i]10 U.S.C. § 2330(b)(3)(C).

Appendix II: Under Secretary of Defense for
Acquisition, Technology, and Logistics
Actions to Address Elements in Section 807 of
the National Defense Authorization Act for
Fiscal Year 2012

[j]Department of Defense Instruction 5000.02, Operation of the Defense Acquisition System Encl. 9, para. 3.e (Dec. 8, 2008).

[k]10 U.S.C. § 2333(e).

Appendix III: Comments from the Department of Defense

OFFICE OF THE UNDER SECRETARY OF DEFENSE
3000 DEFENSE PENTAGON
WASHINGTON, DC 20301-3000

ACQUISITION
TECHNOLOGY
AND LOGISTICS

20 2013

Mr. Timothy J. DiNapoli
Director
Acquisition and Sourcing Management
U.S. Government Accountability Office
441 G Street, N.W.
Washington, DC 20548

Dear Mr. DiNapoli:

This is the Department of Defense's (DoD) response to the GAO Draft Report, GAO-13-634, "DEFENSE AQUISITIONS: Goals and Associated Metrics Needed to Assess Progress in Improving Service Acquisition," dated June 5, 2013 (GAO Code 121087). Comments on the report recommendations are enclosed.

The Department appreciates GAO's work in this important matter. Your report underscores our progress and identifies specific actions that we are taking under a continual improvement initiative, better known as "Better Buying Power". I concur with your recommendations, and they are consistent with ongoing efforts. As our management of services acquisition improves, we should be able to measure performance, track productivity trends, and establish consistent best practices across the Department.

Sincerely,

Richard Ginman
Director, Defense Procurement
and Acquisition Policy

Enclosure:
As stated

GAO Draft Report Dated June 5, 2013
GAO-13-634 (GAO CODE 121087)

"DEFENSE ACQUISITIONS:
Goals and Associated Metrics Needed to Assess Progress in Improving Service Acquisition"

DEPARTMENT OF DEFENSE COMMENTS
TO GAO RECOMMENDATIONS

To better position DOD to determine whether its actions have improved service acquisition, we recommend that the Principal Deputy Under Secretary of Defense for Acquisition, Technology and Logistics, in consultation with the military departments' senior services managers, take the following three actions:

RECOMMENDATION 1: Identify baseline data on the status of service acquisition, in part, by using budget and spending data and leveraging its ongoing efforts to gauge the effects of its actions to improve services acquisitions.

DOD RESPONSE: DOD concurs.

RECOMMENDATION 2: Develop specific goals associated with their actions to improve services acquisitions.

DOD RESPONSE: DOD concurs.

RECOMMENDATION 3: Establish metrics to assess progress in meeting these goals.

DOD RESPONSE: DOD concurs.

Appendix IV: GAO Contact and Staff Acknowledgements

GAO Contact	Timothy J. DiNapoli (202) 512-4841 or dinapolit@gao.gov

Staff Acknowledgments	In addition to the contact name above, the following staff members made key contributions to this report: Johana R. Ayers; Helena Brink, Burns Chamberlain Eckert, Danielle Greene, Kristine Hassinger; Justin Jaynes; and Roxanna Sun.